June 24, 2018

Our Walk With Yeshua

Kaia ~

As you begin this new chapter
of your life, we pray that God would be the
focus of all you do and are. This very
valuable book will help you immeasurably
in that endeavor; not only talking about
the importance of quite and prayer but
also how to deeply study God's most precious
Word that is key in hearing from Him and
allowing Him to guide us and mold us.
Kaia, we love you so much and pray the
Lord would bless you and keep you and
make His face shine upon you and be gracious
to you. We are so excited to see what
God has in store for you!!
Love and Blessings,
Uncle Craig, Aunt Nikki, Caleb, rLondon, Elise, Aliyah

Our Walk With Yeshua

ROBIN HONINGH

Our Walk With Yeshua
Keep searching and finding refreshment in your daily walk with Him

Printed in the United States of America

Correspondence: PO Box 497 Arcadia, IN 46030

ISBN-13: 978-0-692-07815-0

Editor: Charyl Barak
Cover and interior design: Steven Plummer / spbookdesign

ACKNOWLEDGEMENTS

I would first like to thank my Heavenly Father for His faithfulness to me and for His leading me to write this book for such a time as this. I love you my Lord.

I would also like to thank my loving husband Jeroen for his assistance and creativity in the making of this book. Your support has been a great help. Thank you sweetheart.

Thank you to my dear friend Cheryl Barak for editing this book for me. What a wonderful friend and helper God gave me in you. You truly are a blessing.

Thank you to my daughter Kelly for helping me design this book and making helpful suggestions.

To Derek, Shellie, Kelly, Jason, Bobby, Alyssa, Ineke, and Natasha; I love you all and I am proud to be your mother, mother-in-law, and stepmother. You add immense joy to my life.

To my dear mother Loretta and sister Rachel who have supported and prayed for me over the years. A big thank you.

To the many women I have had the privilege of sharing the information found in this book. You have inspired and taught me much over the years. You all know who you are. My deepest thanks. You are all very special to me and are the fruit of my labor.

Finally, I would like to thank my father Junior and grandparents Homer and Florence Hunsinger who are now with the Lord. They instilled in me a desire to know God and to walk with Him by their beautiful example of lives so dedicated to Him. I miss you and think of you often.

TABLE OF CONTENTS

FOREWORD

The beauty of Robin's book *"Our Walk with Yeshua"* is its simplicity. In a world where many of us are overwhelmed with too much information, and many believers have bookcases packed full of excellent books they have no time to read, this short, practical book is a true God-send! It takes the idea of induction, which sounds rather difficult and intimidating, and turns it into something that anyone can do. Thank you, Robin, for consolidating this information and making it available to the body of Yeshua. I believe it will bring depth and richness to many lives.

Helen Mitchell
Author and wife of Elder at Kehilat HaCarmel
Isifiya, Mount Carmel, Israel.

"All Scripture is inspired by God and profitable for teaching, for reproof, for correction, for training in righteousness; so that the man of God may be adequate, equipped for every good work"

2 TIMOTHY 3:16&17

INTRODUCTION

HAVE YOU EVER listened to an anointed sermon or Bible study and wished you could receive knowledge like that from the Lord? Did you think to yourself, "That person must be super spiritual."? Did you wonder how many years they must have studied at Bible college to gain such insight?

Within the pages of this book, you will find a simple process that can radically change the way you relate to God, the way you read and interpret the Bible, and ultimately, the way you walk with the Lord. Throughout this process, you will be guided and directed into spiritual insights you might never have thought possible without years of study. This Bible study method, called induction, coupled with learning to sit and listen to the Lord Himself, can enable you to discover spiritual riches like those you have witnessed in esteemed Bible teachers.

Our pastors have gone through years of study to teach and equip us to follow our Savior. While not everyone is called to the pastorate, all of us are called to draw near to God through our personal walk with Him.

CHAPTER 1
DRYNESS & QUIETNESS

For those of you who have been believers and followers of Yeshua (Jesus) for many years or if you are just beginning your love journey with our Savior, the following pages will enhance your search for continuing refreshment in Yeshua all the days of your life.

Some of us were raised in believing families and have always known about Yeshua, and if you are one of these then it is understandable how daily quiet times can become part of a routine instead of a life-changing daily meeting with the Creator of the world. Unfortunately, many people fall into this category. The treasured information I share with you in the following pages has dramatically changed my life with our Savior. It transformed the dry seasons into incredibly refreshing times directed by the Holy Spirit. It is my prayer that you too, will be forever changed as you venture into this journey with our Lord.

It is very important to enter into a daily quiet time void of confusion and noise. *"For thus the Lord God, The Holy One of Israel, has said, 'In repentance and rest you will be saved, in quietness and trust is our strength.'"* (Isaiah 30:15). Once you find that special time each day to be with your Lord, ask God to lead you to a special worship song to start your time with Him. Worship plows the heart, making it fertile and ready to receive what God has for you in His Word that day. A common Hebrew word for worship (nishtachave) means to bow oneself down. A common Greek word for worship (proskuneo) means to kiss the hand. Worship in the true scriptural sense is not passive. We need to be purposeful in our quiet times with the Lord, especially in worship, as it is the beginning of intimacy with our Lord. We have a tendency to go to God and immediately start asking Him for all we need. I remember when my children were little, they would sometimes burst into the room early in the morning screeching, "Mommy, Mommy, I need…" without so much as a, "Hi Mom, how are you? I love you Mommy". I wonder how many times we do this to our heavenly Daddy in our prayer life?

CHAPTER 2
ACTS ACRONYM

AN ACRONYM THAT has revolutionized many prayer lives is ACTS – A is for Acclamation, C is for Confession, T is for Thanksgiving, and S is for Supplication.

Acclamation

Make it a habit to use this order when meeting with your Lord each day. Begin by spending some time in *acclamation*, and just praise Him for who He is. In this step, do not praise Him for what He has done for you, but simply for all He is, your All in All. Isaiah, chapter 6, is an awesome place to find a description of what the throne room of God looks like and of some of the activity that goes on there. Imagine yourself standing before God and realizing how small you are when you are in His presence. What a gift this experience was for

Isaiah, and what a gift it is for us as well! (I seldom enter into a worship time without first thinking of myself walking into His Throne room from the Isaiah 6 picture.) I see myself for who I really am every time I enter His Throne room in my mind and heart. Now, imagine yourself walking up to the Lord and worshipping Him by bowing down before Him and kissing His hand, the hand that was voluntarily pierced out of love for you. This adds a whole new intimacy to our quiet time. It brings us into a deeper personal relationship with our Messiah.

Confession

In this frame of mind, move on to *confession.* Get yourself in right standing before the Father through our Savior's blood, which was shed for our iniquities. Yeshua has made it possible for us to enter into the Holy of Holies, a place we were never allowed to go before. He paid the penalty for our sins and rent the veil between the Holy and Most Holy place in the tabernacle. (Matt. 27:50-51) How His red blood and my black sin can equal a clean, white, forgiven man or woman is beyond all understanding. It would be impossible without our Lord Yeshua's sacrifice.

BLACK SIN
+
RED BLOOD
=
WHITE, CLEAN
AND FORGIVEN

Thanksgiving

The next and most natural step is *thanksgiving*. This is the step where we can praise Him for what He has done for us. We have so much to be thankful for after thinking and praying through these first two steps. Yeshua paid the ultimate price for you and me, and He did it willingly. Speak the things you are thankful for. Speak them out loud to your Lord.

Supplication

The last step, which we usually make our first step, is *supplication*. So many times, after going through these first three steps, I find that the supplications I first thought I needed to ask for have changed. Being in the presence of God alters the way we see our circumstances and needs. The Holy Spirit also has had time in the first three steps to show us what we need to pray for and what His will is. Like the example of my young children rushing into my room with their demands and desires, instead of first greeting me and showing me respect and love, we too, tend to rush into the throne room of God without giving proper respect and love to the God of the universe, the King of Kings, the Lord of Lords and our personal Savior. Make a deliberate effort to change these habits into times which honor our Lord. When my children came in and hugged me, loved me, and showed me how much respect they had for me, it set a deep, meaningful time together in motion. Our Lord deserves that from us, and so much more. And He is just waiting to show us His love every time we come to Him.

Listening

Personally, I like to add a fifth step to the ACTS acronym and it is *listening*. I always give a challenge to women, to give God one full minute after praying through the above steps. Quiet yourself and give Him just one minute of your time with your head cleared of everything else and let Him whisper in your ear. These have been minutes that have changed the course of my life many times. You will get so tuned into His voice that you will recognize it more easily and more quickly than you did before. He has spoken words of wisdom in my ear, directed me to particular Scriptures, and assured me of His guidance. I let Him have full reign over this minute to teach me in a way that only He can. When this type of communion with God happens, it is miraculous!

CHAPTER 3

INTRODUCTION OF INDUCTION AND PRAYER

WHILE ATTENDING MOODY Bible Institute in Chicago, Illinois, I attended a class entitled, "Elements of Bible Study" otherwise known as *Induction*. It changed my life! My prayer for you at this time is that it will change yours as well. I would like to take a moment right now and pray for you and your time in this book.

Our precious Lord, I pray that this time and these efforts of your servant are directed and guided by the Holy Spirit. I pray for the understanding and counsel only You can give, to make us more like Yeshua our Messiah. Thank You Lord that You care about us so much and that You have given us Your Holy Word as a lamp unto our feet and a light unto our path. I thank You that You give us a tender and passionate heart for You. Grow us into a deeper walk with You as a result of our time in Your Word. Holy Spirit, lead us into special times at the feet of our Lord. In Yeshua's mighty name we pray. Amen.

❦

This method of Bible study called induction, has drawn many people into a closer walk with Jesus. A walk that is more intimate than ever thought possible. One of the primary purposes of induction is to draw your attention to details. We drive places all the time and hardly notice the things that we pass. For example, take a minute and try to recall five specific things that you saw the last time you drove somewhere. How many can you remember?

One exercise that is a good start to induction is to

HOLY SPIRIT,

lead us into

SPECIAL TIMES

at the

FEET OF OUR LORD.

put an object in the middle of a table, (I like to use one of those Russian Matryoshka dolls that have several dolls nesting inside one another). Grab a piece of paper and write down in one minute all the things you notice while looking at the object. Then for one more minute pick it up and examine it a little closer to see what else you can discover. It is amazing what we do not notice in normal situations but when we closely observe something even for just two minutes, we have a whole page of details! Try this exercise for yourself. The results are the same with Bible study. We read as we normally read, but when we examine the subject more closely it is absolutely amazing the things we find that we never saw before. Induction teaches us how to find the deeper, spiritual gold nuggets that we might have otherwise overlooked.

When I first attended a Bible study in which the teacher used induction as the method of study for preparation, I approached her after class and said, "I have been a Christian most of my life and I have never heard the information from the book of John that you shared with us tonight. How did you discover these things?" I saw more in the Word of God than I had ever seen before and it instilled a hunger in me that has never diminished to this day. This is the reason I am writing this book, so others can also have their hunger stimulated in a way never thought possible. Since 1999 I have studied inductively and have taught many women this method of study. Something I have heard repeatedly that breaks my heart is, "I am so hungry to go deeper but I don't know how". The Lord instructed me, not long ago, to write this information down and distribute it so more women can feast more deeply than just the number I am able to personally teach. Right now, I am writing as I sit on top of Mount Carmel in Israel. My husband and I spend three months of every year here in the Holy Land ministering for our Lord. I have learned so much about intimacy with Him while walking and listening on this mountain. It was while spending time with Him here that He instructed me to write this down to share with as many as He instructs me to. What a privilege and honor it is to walk with Him and pay close attention to His instructions. Fruit will grow as we spend time with Him and learn from His Word. I pray that you are part of that fruit that grows from this book.

"Study to shew thyself approved unto God,

a workman that needeth not to be ashamed,

rightly dividing the word of truth".

2 TIMOTHY 2:15 (KING JAMES VERSION)

CHAPTER 4
THREE STEPS

HERE **WE GO** - Three Steps of Induction
There are 3 steps of induction:

1. Observation – What does it say?

2. Interpretation – What does it mean?

3. Application – What does it mean to me?

I will explain each step and allow you to have a chance to practice each one before teaching you the next one.

CHAPTER 5

OBSERVATION

Step One: Observation

THERE ARE THREE steps in the inductive method, the first one being observation. We talked a little about this with the doll exercise. In observation, we want to read a portion or book of Scripture several times and like the doll exercise, we want to write down what we observe in order to understand what it says. The more you read the passage, the more you will see in it. Read it in different versions of the Scriptures, read it out loud, listen to it online, etc. You want to pay attention to the five W's: *Who, What, When, Where, and Why.*

Who wrote the book and who did they write it to? *What* is happening in this particular situation? Also look into what was happening in the whole book even if you are reading just a portion. *When* was this particular book written? *Where* was the writer of the book when he wrote it and where were the recipients? *Why* did the author choose to write at this particular time to these particular people in that particular place?

Remember these 5 "W's" as you are reading a book or particular section of Scripture. It is important to completely understand and keep things in the perspective of what God was communicating to those people at that time. The more time you spend in observation, the more accurate your interpretation will be. A correct interpretation is so important, yet is often neglected. Without a correct interpretation, the meaning of what God is trying to say to us can be misunderstood and can become a "different gospel", something God warns us to avoid (Galatians 1:8). As you use this kind of observation, God will begin speaking to you in ways that you have never imagined. He will honor you as you honor His Holy Word. This is very different than just reading it; it is becoming a student of His Holiness and discovering who He is at a much deeper and more intimate level.

If you would like an example exercise to put your new skill into practice before moving onto interpretation, try the following: Pray and ask God where He wants you to read in His Word. Let Him confirm to you where He is intending you to read. For the sake of this exercise, I am going to give you a recommendation but certainly follow God's guidance if He instructs you to read somewhere else. Be sure to look closely at what you are reading and read it several times. I was once advised by a teacher who was inducting the book of Esther with us to read it fifty times in the month before we began the class. Her students came with so much information and were ready to delve deeply into the book. It was fantastic. Notice things as you read. When you see a "therefore", find out what it is there for! If you are reading a chapter to observe, read the verses or chapter preceding it for an explanation of what it is there for. If you read, "the next day", find out what happened the day before. Where were they? What were they doing there? Also notice key people in the passage or book. Who are they?

There is a book entitled, "Living by the Book", by Howard Hendricks, who in my opinion, was one of the greatest teachers of induction and God's Word. Maybe you've heard of him. If you would like to read an in-depth teaching on induction, order his book. It is an excellent resource. The following is an experiment out of "Living by the Book"

Read the entire book of Esther every day for a week. Read it in different versions, read it out loud, or perhaps

Let the **HOLY SPIRIT**, *teach you as you* **SATURATE** *yourself with the* **WORD.**

listen to it on a Bible application on your phone. Observe, observe, observe. As you read, write down questions you may have. Questions you might not have considered before. Write down who the main characters are, repeated words, and other items of interest. Anything you observe, jot it down. See how many new things you can discover each day. Make a list of your observations or write them in your Bible. Imagine living the lives of the characters you are reading about and how their circumstances impacted their lives. You will be amazed at what you will discover that you never saw before. Ask yourself what insights you have gained from the story. At the end of the week, see if you can reconstruct the story clearly and accurately by telling it to someone else. If you are a mother, tell it to your children, if you're a grandmother, share it with your grandchildren, maybe you have a friend you can spend some time with and tell him or her.[1]

Let the Holy Spirit teach you as you saturate yourself with the Word. John 1:1 says, "In the beginning was the Word, and the Word was with God, and the Word was God". When we saturate ourselves with God's Word we are actually filling ourselves with Yeshua Himself. Understanding this adds importance to spending time reading the Bible. Be sure to set aside

---

1 Howard Hendricks, William Hendricks. (1991). *Living by the Book*. Chicago: Moody Press.Used by permission.

CHAPTER 6

INTERPRETATION

Step Two: Interpretation

IN INTERPRETATION, WE are answering the question, "What does this mean?". Accuracy is crucial in this step. The five "W's" need to be answered and the answers written down on paper before this step is completed. Repeated words, cause and effect words such as: but, therefore, then, now it happened, etc., should also be written down. I like to put the five "W" facts on a small postcard for quick reference to help me keep an accurate perspective as I study. This will be the foundation of your information and you will continue to build upon it. Once you determine when the book was written, do a little investigating and find out what else was going on in the world at that time. This broadens your perspective and helps you determine why this particular book or portion was written at this particular time in history. The internet is a great place to look for this type of information, but choose your websites carefully. They need to be reliable and trustworthy. They also need to have a godly perspective to aid our understanding. To find out more about a person or people group, you can use a Bible dictionary which can be found in hard copies or on the internet. One of my favorites is the Holman Bible Dictionary but there are many good ones available. If you are in question as to which are trustworthy, look at the publishers. This is a good way to know what denomination the book is affiliated with and also to know how reliable the book may or may not be. When I see publishers such as: Zondervan, Tyndale, or Moody, I feel confident as these companies have stood the test of time. You can also find Bible locations in Bible dictionaries and Bible handbooks. Sometimes these materials include maps so you can see the location of the writer in relation to his recipients. Knowing the surrounding areas is informative and helpful. Blueletterbible.org is a website that has many Bible helping books and also includes a Strong's Concordance. I would strongly encourage you to avoid Bible commentaries until you have concluded your own induction study. This way you will not settle for what someone else's induction study revealed, but you will make your own discoveries. I like to consult a

Bible commentary after I have done my study to see if my results are similar to what Bible scholars have found.

One of the most helpful books is a Strong's Exhaustive Concordance. Over the years, cultures and languages change, and meanings of words change as well. Unless you understand Greek (New Testament language) and Hebrew (Old Testament language) it is hard to know the precise meanings of the words. History and culture play a significant part in understanding the usage of words. Strong's Concordance contains a dictionary of the Bible and its original languages. You can see why this is so important for induction. Many Strong's Concordances are written to work with the King James version of the Bible so it is important to have access to a King James version when conducting your studies. I have come across words that mean the exact opposite of what I know they mean in my English language. A good example is found in Psalm 21:3 using the King James version. "Thou preventest him with the blessings of goodness: thou settest a crown of pure gold on his head". The word "prevent" is usually associated with hindrance, but here in this Scripture, it actually means to precede, to fulfill in advance, to anticipate, to pay a debt before it is due. With the correct meaning which is found in the Strong's Concordance, this verse means that God is anxious to bless us and looks forward to us asking Him for our needs. Another good reason to use the Strong's Concordance is to discover how many meanings a particular word has in Hebrew or Greek. Love, for example, is several different words in the Hebrew and Greek languages and these words have different meanings. It must be determined which meaning the author is using in each instance in order to understand exactly what he is trying to convey.

I will also give you a modern-day example of this. When I was younger and someone said that something was bad, I knew that meant negative or even dangerous. My grandson and I were sitting on the porch not long ago and a sports car went by and he said, "Grandma, that car is so bad.", meaning it was very pleasing to him. Same word but a completely different meaning. What happened to change that meaning? Time and culture, (and that is just in the American English language over a span of fifty years). When we read the Scriptures, we are reading words from thousands of years ago, from different cultures, and different languages. Imagine how distorted our understanding might be. This is why a Strong's Concordance is vital to serious Bible study. I have been a Christian most of my life, yet not until I was thirty years old did I know what a Strong's Concordance was. I have found it to be an incredible tool and one that greatly enhanced my life with the Lord. While you are doing your induction studies, write down which resource book you found your information in with the corresponding page number. This saves you from having to find it again later. Trust me, I speak from experience and want to save you from this frustration.

Some probing questions you can ask during the interpretation step are: What does the author mean, think, see, or feel to make him write this way? Why did he write it? What would it mean to the people of his time and culture? Again, I would like to emphasize the importance of reading what is written before and after the portion you are studying. Context is very important. What does this mean in regard to the rest of the Bible? Also, consider what is not written there. Why might the author leave certain information out of his narrative? Remember, that the authors of the Bible used familiar settings and subjects, often right in front of them, when writing. These things would be familiar to their audience and therefore would be easy to understand. For example, the apostle Paul, when he wrote about the armor of God in Ephesians 6, was under house arrest and being guarded by a Roman guard. What did Roman guards wear? If you research Roman guard armor in the first century A.D. and study the different pieces of armor, you will understand the great spiritual similarities Paul was writing about. This was a real-life situation and he used it to teach about the kingdom of God. Can you imagine Paul sitting on his chair writing his letter to the Ephesians and possibly sharing with the guard what he was describing to the believers in Ephesus? Do you think it would have made an impact on this guard? When he put on his uniform the following day do you think his encounter with Paul would have gone through his mind while getting dressed? Think about it. We know of other instances in the Bible when guards came to salvation because of believers sharing their faith with them while imprisoned. Now, let us think about the people that received Paul's letter. We have determined that they were in Ephesus. If you look up Ephesus in a Bible dictionary, you will find that they too knew what Roman guard uniforms consisted of and could relate to the spiritual application Paul was making. You can take this a step further and study each piece of armor to discover each particular use. When you study this way, you will not forget what you have learned, and the Holy Spirit can use the importance of what it actually meant in that culture and help you apply these lessons to your life.

Take some time now and apply these interpretation skills to the scriptures you observed in step one. If you chose the book of Esther use it. If not then use whatever God led you to. Look into the Bible helping books described in this chapter and write down all your findings. Enjoy this journey!

CHAPTER 7

APPLICATION

Step 3 Application

IN THIS FINAL and important step, we come to understand what the Scriptures mean to us personally but only after we have understood what God was communicating to a particular people at a particular point in history. Without proper interpretation, we can make the Bible mean almost anything we want it to mean. So be sure you have completed proper interpretation before moving on to application.

Ask the following questions to discover your application: Is there an example to follow? A sin to forsake? A promise to claim? A command I should obey? These are the first steps in application and are the easiest to find. These general application truths should be found throughout the Bible; meaning you should be able to apply them to principles that God has written else-where in His Word. Once you find these, spend some time alone with God going through the ACTS pro-cess of prayer. With the general applications that you have written down, ask God, "How does this apply to me right now?" For example, if you found a promise to claim, how does that promise fit into your life in what you are presently experiencing? For example, you might have found the promise, "I will never leave you nor forsake you", and just yesterday you received some negative news about your job.

You have to make the decision to trust God no matter what happens and this particular promise from your induction study speaks deeply into your heart. You know that God will never leave you nor forsake you even in the midst of your difficulty. As you spend time with Him in prayer and apply that final step of listening for one minute (which was discussed earlier in this book), He may lead you to other verses that also give you instructions on how He wants to walk you through this situation in your life. There are many ways He speaks to us. Sometimes it is a still small voice in our heart, sometimes He speaks to us through a sermon or a friend, He can talk to you through a wor-ship song or some other means. Not arriving at the conclusion of what the Scriptures mean personally to us, is like abandoning ship before we even realize how strong the ship is. When God makes these intimate connections with you, you will experience a whole new relationship with Him. He will become your best friend and constant companion. A companion that you know will never leave you nor forsake you.

Now spend some time applying these application skills to the scriptures you have observed and interpreted up to this point. This final step is where lives are changed. Make sure and write out your applications, then pray and listen for Gods responses to you. The last step in this process is to write down what God wants you to do as a response to your personal application. I encourage you to keep a list of ways God is changing your life as you learn and practice induction.

CHAPTER 8
CHALLENGE

I HAVE OFTEN CHALLENGED women to ask God to show them a personal life verse, one that He has especially for them. (At different times in my life I have added other verses as I go through different seasons.) I then encourage the women to induct their life verses to find the true meaning of what that verse meant to the people to whom it was written and then apply it to their own lives after they have found the correct interpretation. I guarantee you that the meaning of your verse will be experienced more deeply when you do this. It is a beautiful thing to have an intimate verse between you and your Lord.

After my husband learned induction he said the following: "What I like about the inductive process of Bible study is that it doesn't only apply to the Word of

God but eventually you start to look at your own life through this process as well. You look at the things that have happened in the past and the things that are happening in the present and you think about those things inductively. You begin to see more clearly how God sees you, how God uses you, and how God loves you. There are many things about this process of Bible study that go much deeper than traditional Bible study. It becomes part of your life and the way life should be viewed".

I pray that as you think through this book and apply it to your life, it will take you deeper into a love relationship with your Lord and Savior. I pray you will never be the same again as a result. At the beginning of the book I encouraged you to ask God to lead you to worship songs before you begin your time with Him each day. This will open your heart to receive from Him. According to the Scriptures when the children of Israel gathered together for worship, it was the Levitical worshipers that led the Lord's people into His presence. I believe worship has the power to do the same for us. This, followed by the study of God's Word through the induction process you have just learned, will find you in the throne room of God, experiencing His presence like never before.

SUGGESTED READINGS

Living by the Book
by Howard and William Hendricks

Journey into God's Word
by Scott Duvall and Daniel Hays

Signposts & Waymarks
by Helen Mitchell

PERSONAL NOTES

PERSONAL NOTES

PERSONAL NOTES

PERSONAL NOTES